The Funny Zone

HISTORY ZONE

Read Jokes. Write Jokes.

Jokes, Riddles, Tongue Twisters & "Daffynitions"

By Gary Chmielewski

Illustrated by Jim Caputo

Ha! Ha! Ha! Ha! Ha! Ha! Ha! Ha! Ha! Ha! Ha! Ha!

A Note to Caregivers and Educators:

As the old saying goes, "Laughter is the best medicine." It's true for reading as well. Kids naturally love humor, so why not look to their interests to get them motivated to read? The Funny Zone series features books that include jokes, riddles, word plays, and tongue twisters – all of which are sure to delight your young reader.

We invite you to share this book with your child, taking turns to read aloud to one another, practicing timing, emphasis, and expression. You and your child can deliver the jokes in a natural voice, or have fun creating character voices and exaggerating funny words. Be sure to pause often to make sure your child understands the jokes. Talk about what you are reading and use this opportunity to explore new vocabulary words and ideas. Reading aloud can help your child build confidence in reading.

Along with being fun and motivating, humorous text involves higher order thinking skills that support comprehension. Jokes, riddles, and word plays require us to explore the creative use of language, develop word and sound recognition, and expand vocabulary.

At the end of the book are activities to help your child develop writing skills. These activities tap your child's creativity by exploring numerous types of humor.

Above all, the most important part of the reading experience is to have fun and enjoy it!

Sincerely,

Shannon Cannon

Shannon Cannon, Ph.D.
Literacy Consultant

NORWOOD HOUSE PRESS

P.O. Box 316598 • Chicago, Illinois 60631
For information regarding Norwood House Press, please visit our website at: www.norwoodhousepress.com or call 866-565-2900.

Designer: Design Lab
Project Management: Editorial Directions

Library of Congress Cataloging-in-Publication Data:
Chmielewski, Gary, 1946–
   The history zone / by Gary Chmielewski ; illustrated by Jim Caputo.
      p. cm. — (The funny zone series)
Summary: "Contains history-themed jokes for children as well as exercises to teach children how to write their own jokes"—Provided by publisher.
   ISBN-13: 978-1-59953-141-0 (library edition : alk. paper)
   ISBN-10: 1-59953-141-0 (library edition : alk. paper)
   1. History—Juvenile humor. 2. Wit and humor, Juvenile. 3. Jokes. I. Caputo, Jim. II. Title.
D10.C485 2008
902'.07—dc22   2007015390

Hardcover ISBN: 978-1-59953-141-0   Paperback ISBN: 978-1-60357-678-9

313R—012018
Manufactured in the United States of America in North Mankato, Minnesota.

ANCIENT TIMES

If Atlas supported the world on his shoulders, who supported Atlas?

His wife!

What do Alexander the Great and Kermit the Frog have in common?

Their middle name!

All the best, Kermit

Teacher: "What was the name of the person in Greek mythology who was half man and half animal?"

Sandy: "Buffalo Bill."

3

Who was the biggest thief in history?

Atlas, he held up the whole world!

Diane: "Crystal, when was Rome built?"

Crystal: "At night!"

Diane: "What do you mean at night?"

Crystal: "Don't you know that Rome wasn't built in a day?"

How was the Roman Empire cut in half?

With a pair of Caesars!

Teacher: "What is a forum?"

Lisa: "Two-um plus two-um!"

Teacher: "What did Caesar say to Cleopatra?"

Casey: "Toga-ether we can rule the world!"

Teacher: "What was the greatest accomplishment of the early Romans?"

Rick: "Speaking Latin!"

Teacher: "Christy, who succeeded the First Emperor of Rome?"

Christy: "The second one!"

Teacher: "When did Caesar reign?"

Yolanda: "I didn't know he reigned."

Teacher: "Of course he did, didn't they hail him?"

Teacher: "What is the 1286BC inscribed on the mummy's tomb?"

Laura: "The license number of the car that hit him!"

Teacher: "Did they play tennis in ancient Egypt?"

Jimmy: "Yes, Joseph served in Pharaoh's court!"

Teacher: "What can you tell me about the Dead Sea?"

Abe: "Dead? I didn't even know it was sick!"

Teacher: "Why did Julius Caesar buy crayons?"

Daniel: "He wanted to Marc Antony!"

EUROPE

Why were the early days of history called the 'Dark Ages'?
Because there were so many knights!

Teacher: "When a knight was killed in battle, what sign did they put on his grave?"

Anna: "Rust In Peace!"

RUST
IN
PEACE

Why is England the wettest country in the world?

Because the queen has reigned there for years!

"Night, night, knight," said one knight to the other knight the other night!

7

Who made King Arthur's round table?

Sir Cumference!

What King invented fractions?

Henry the 1/8th!

Camelot

A place people parked their camels!

CAMELOT

1 HR. = 1 SILVER
8 HRS. = 5 SILVER
1 DAY = 2 GOLD

What did the Sheriff of Nottingham say when Robin Hood fired at him?

"That was an arrow escape!"

Professor: "Why did King Arthur have a round table?"

Antonio: "So no one could corner him!"

When was King Arthur's army too tired to fight?

When they had lots of sleepless knights!

What was the first thing Queen Elizabeth did on ascending to the throne?

Sat down!

Professor: "Why did Robin Hood only rob from the rich?"

Amanda: "The poor didn't have anything worth stealing!"

9

How does a king open a door?

With a monar-chy

What do you call a king's sore throat?

A royal pain-in-the-neck!

RING-A-LING!
RING-A-LING!

History's a subject that's
As dead as it can be.
Once it killed the Romans,
And now it's killing me.

How do you see King Arthur after it gets dark?

With a knight light!

COMING TO AMERICA

Kathleen sat down to eat in an ice cream parlor. Her dog sat in the chair beside her.

"Sorry," said the waiter. "Dogs aren't allowed in here."

"But this is a talking dog," Kathleen said.

"If the dog can talk, I'll give you a free banana split," offered the waiter.

Kathleen turned to the dog and asked, "When did Columbus come to America?"

"Gr-rrrrrr'" growled the dog.

"I knew he couldn't talk," said the waiter. "Now scram!"

Outside on the sidewalk, the dog looked up at Kathleen and asked, "Should I have said 1492?"

What did the Pilgrims say when Squanto showed them how to grow corn?

"That's a-maize-ing!"

Teacher: "Ben, what happened in the year 1492?"

Ben: "I don't know. I wasn't alive back then."

Teacher: "I'll give you a hint. Do Nina, Pinta, and Santa Maria sound familiar?"

Ben: "Not to me. I don't know a lot about salsa music!"

Teacher: "Where did the Pilgrims land when they came to America?"

Jade: "On their feet!"

Why did the Pilgrims' pants always fall down?

They wore their belt buckles on their hats!

THE REVOLUTIONARY WAR AND THE CONSTITUTION

What did Paul Revere say at the end of his famous ride?

"WHOA!"

Teacher: "What did they do at the Boston Tea Party?"
Brianna: "I don't know, I wasn't invited!"

Darrell: "A duck family must have given the Liberty Bell to Philadelphia."
Emily: "Why a duck family?"
Darrell: "Didn't you say there was a quack in it?"

Headmaster: "What did they wear to the Boston Tea Party?"
Aaron: "T-shirts!"

What did Paul Revere say when he got on his horse?

"Giddy up horsey!"

13

What's the difference between Paul Revere and Sir Lancelot?

Paul Revere was a nightrider, and Sir Lancelot was a knight rider!

What did Betsy Ross say when they asked if the flag was ready?

"Just give me a Minute, Man!"

Ms. Howland: "Amanda, could you please tell the class what you know about the Second Amendment to the Constitution."

Amanda: "Certainly. The Second Amendment is the one that says we can pull up our sleeves."

Ms. Howland: "That's a strange answer."

Amanda: "Why? Doesn't it say that we have the right to bare arms?"

19TH CENTURY AMERICA

What did Mason say to Dixon?

"We've got to draw the line here!"

In what battle did General Wolfe cry, "I die happy!"?

His last one!

Knock, Knock.

Who's there?

O'Shea.

O'Shea who?

O'Shea can you see, by the dawn's early light.

PRESIDENTS

What did John Adams become when he was 41 years old?

A year older on his birthday!

Why did George Washington chop down the cherry tree?

Teacher: "Abraham Lincoln had a very hard childhood. He walked 8 miles to school every day!"

Felicia: "Well, he should have gotten up earlier. Then he could ride a school bus like everyone else!"

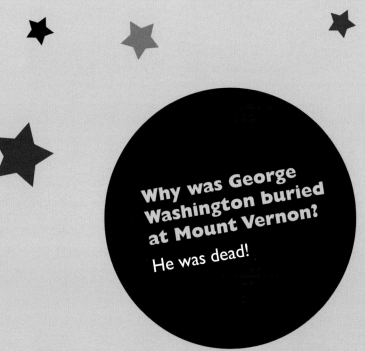

Why was George Washington buried at Mount Vernon?

He was dead!

Teacher: "Sarah, what was Abraham Lincoln most famous for?"

Sarah: "His memory."

Teacher: "His memory? Why would you say that?"

Sarah: "Because in Washington, D.C., there is a monument to Lincoln's memory."

Teacher: "Jake, what important historical event happened in 1809?"

Jake: "Abraham Lincoln was born."

Teacher: "Correct. Now tell me—what important historical event took place in 1812?"

Jake: "Lincoln celebrated his third birthday."

Teacher: "Dwayne, I am disappointed in the results of your history test. When I was your age, I knew the names of all the presidents."

Dwayne: "Yes, but there were so few presidents then."

AMERICAN WEST

What did Pony Express riders ride in the dark?

Nightmares!

Teacher: "Why did the pioneers cross the country in covered wagons?"

Tamika: "They didn't want to wait 40 years for the train!"

Helen: "How did you do on your tests?"

Russ: "I did what General Custer did."

Helen: "What's that?"

Russ: "I went down in history!"

Charles: "Can you spell 'house' with only two letters?"

Kevin: "No. How can you spell 'house' with only two letters?"

Charles: "T-P."

Teacher: "Nathan, who won at Bull Run?"

Nathan: "I don't know – was the score in the papers?"

HISTORY LESSONS

Why does history keep repeating itself?
Because we weren't listening the first time!

David: " I wish I had been born 100 years ago!"
Hannah: "Why is that?"
David: "Just think of all the history that I wouldn't have to learn!"

Teacher: "Why are you reading the last pages of your history book first?"

Philip: "I want to know how it ends!"

Teacher: "Cody, name one important thing we have today that we didn't have 100 years ago."

Cody: "Me!"

Gabrielle: "What's so hard about history class?"

Lisa: "The teacher keeps asking me about things that happened before I was born."

What do history teachers make when they want to get together?

Dates!

Patrick: "I'm learning history!"

Abe: "So am I. Let's go for a walk and talk about old times!"

"It's clear," said the teacher, "that you haven't studied your history. Tina, what's your excuse?"

"Well, my dad says 'our world is changing every day'. So I decided to wait until it settles down."

"Miss Fergus, the world is square, not round," said Brent.

"No, the world is round, Brent. Who told you it was square?" replied the teacher.

"My older sister Emily. She claims she's been to all 4 corners of the earth."

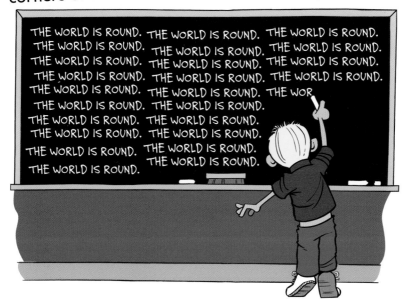

History Teacher: "Dave, when did the Great Depression take place?"

Dave: "After I brought home my report card."

Maria: "Tell me, Brent, why did you fail history?"

Brent: "I just don't understand it. Everything the history teacher says goes in both ears and out the other."

Maria: "But that's three ears!"

Brent: "I'm not doing very well in arithmetic either."

What do historians talk about when they meet?

Old times, of course!

How do you fire a science teacher?

Tell her she's history!

Kristen: "I studied history for four hours last night and I still flunked the test."

Travis: "Do you have any idea why?"

Kristen: "I guess it was because the test was on math."

Erin: "Mike, will you tutor me in history?"

Mike: "I'll be glad to, but I charge 75 cents for every two questions you want answered."

Erin: "Isn't that expensive?"

Mike: "Yes it is. What is your second question?"

WRITING JOKES CAN BE AS MUCH FUN AS READING THEM!

Knock knock jokes are fun to write. They always begin the same way. You say "Knock, knock" and the other person says, "Who's there?" The next lines are plays on words. This means that you use words in funny ways so people will laugh. For example, take a look at the knock knock joke on page 15:

> Knock, knock.
> Who's there?
> O'Shea.
> O'Shea who?
> O'Shea can you see, by the dawn's early light.

This joke is funny because it uses the last name O'Shea to substitute for the words "O say" in the first line of The Star Spangled Banner.

YOU TRY IT!

STEP 1: Make a list of names of some people or places that you know.

STEP 2: Read each one out loud. Does the name remind you of anything else? Does it sound like another word? Does it sound like another word or group of words if you say it quickly? If it does, circle the word and write down the words it sounds like or reminds you of. Go through your entire list.

STEP 3: Next, put all the words you selected in knock knock form. For example, the name Shirley and the word surely sound alike, but mean different things. When made into a knock knock joke it would go like this:

> Knock, knock.
> Who's there?
> Shirley
> Shirley who?
> Shirley you know who this is!

STEP 4: Write down all the knock knock jokes you can think of, even the ones that don't make you laugh out loud.

STEP 5: Finally, try out your jokes on someone else. If you want to be extra sure they are funny, try them out on someone who hardly ever laughs. If he or she laughs, then you know you have mastered the art of knock knock joke writing!

Don't stop here!

Collect your jokes in a journal and share with your family and friends when they need a good laugh!